Outback Adventures

Jim Cromarty

© Copyright 2004 Jim Cromarty
ISBN 978-1-85792-974-4
Reprinted in 2007
by
Christian Focus Publications,
Geanies House, Fearn, Tain
Ross-shire, IV20 1TW,
Great Britain

Cover design by Alister Macinnes
Cover illustration by Graham Kennedy
Maps and other illustrations by Fred Apps

Printed in Great Britain
by CPD, Wales

Contents

Australia

A ustralia is a huge island found between the Pacific and
Indian Oceans. In 1770 James Cook, the captain of
the *Endeavour,* took possession of the land for the King of
Great Britain, thus *The Great South Land* became part of the
British Empire. Today, Australia is one of many nations
linked to Great Britain as an independent member of the
Commonwealth of Nations.

Justice in England was very severe. In the days of William
Shakespeare some crimes resulted in the offender being boiled
alive for all to see. People who stole property valued at more
than 5/- (five shillings) were hanged. Crowds of people would
bring their meal with them when they set out to watch the
latest criminal being plunged into eternity on the gallows.
Many criminals were sentenced to lengthy prison terms in
one of the colonies. In 1776 the USA became an independent
nation, with the result that they refused to accept any more
British criminals. Consequently the decision was made to
transport thousands to Australia.

On 13 May, 1787 Governor Phillip, with a fleet of twelve
ships, set out to establish a settlement in Australia. The fleet

that sailed from England carried five hundred and sixty four male convicts, one hundred and ninety two women and thirteen infants belonging to the convicts. In all, counting soldiers, guards, doctors and others, one thousand and seventeen people left Great Britain to establish a convict settlement in the "Land Down Under." The fleet arrived in Australia in 1788. Today in Australia there is a degree of pride at being able to trace one's ancestry to a convict who was transported on the first fleet.

Before the settlement took place, the huge island was occupied by many aboriginal tribes, who were given no say in what happened in 1770 and 1788.

The land was soon divided into six states named New South Wales, Queensland, Victoria, South Australia, Western Australia and later what was called Northern Territory. To the south is the island state of Tasmania. On 1 January, 1901 the states united to form the Commonwealth of Australia. For a time there was a dispute between the governments of New South Wales and Victoria concerning the state where the Commonwealth Government would meet. This was solved when New South Wales set aside a portion of land which is known as the Australian Capital Territory (A.C.T.) with Canberra as the seat of government.

Australia is 7,686,848 square kilometres in size. From east to west it measures 3,983 kilometres, and from north to south 3,138 kilometres. The coastline measures 27,948 kilometres which includes Tasmania and the 821 small islands dotted along Australia's coastline. Our highest mountain is Mount

Kosciusko which rises to 2,228 metres above sea level, while Lake Eyre in parts is sixteen metres below sea level. Australia has a national Coat of Arms - a shield decorated with the state badges which is supported by an emu and a kangaroo. Both of these animals cannot walk backwards, which symbolises a nation that is ever moving forward. In 2002 the population was estimated to be close to 20,000,000.

Christians should be people who walk forward, following God's ways. Christians shouldn't retreat and in God's strength they should keep following in his ways. God's Word the Bible teaches his people how to live and Jesus himself has told them not to give up. 'No one who puts his hand to the plough and looks back is fit for the kingdom of God.' Luke 9:62.

In Australia most people live along the coastal plains where the rainfall is sufficient to support the population and provide adequate water to grow the crops needed to support both animal and human life. Once we cross the Great Dividing Range the land becomes drier. The interior desert regions are of no real value for agriculture. The land far beyond the Great Dividing Range is *The Australian Outback*.

The convict settlers worked in the coastal areas but, with the arrival of free settlers and with released convicts, the move inland commenced. The outback was settled by courageous men and women who claimed their piece of land. Many established cattle and sheep stations, while others concentrated on wheat production.

It was the inland that provided the best land for sheep because of the low rainfall. Wet weather along the coast had caused the crippling foot rot amongst the sheep.

The wheat that was first grown along the coastal areas suffered from a disease called rust, causing the wheat farmers to move over the Great Dividing Range to the western plains where there was good weather for both cattle, sheep and wheat.

However the inland area had great tracts of land with a low rainfall. In many places the land selected as a station for sheep or cattle was little better than desert. This meant that many hectares of land were needed to feed just one animal. The sheep and beef cattle had to compete with thousands of kangaroos for the small amount of pastures available. However, the settlers discovered that when the rain did fall, the deserts bloomed with a multitude of coloured flowers and pastures grew for the animals to eat.

Those early settlers found life very difficult. They travelled in carts which carried everything needed to clear the land, build houses, till the soil, as well as seed to grow vegetables for themselves, and crops to feed the cattle and sheep. In addition they had herds of cattle to drive before them to the land they were to claim as their own. Imagine, if you can, Dad and his family, workmen, herds of cattle or sheep facing thick bushland and a range of mountains. To reach the outback regions it meant cutting a pathway through the timber. The newcomers had to be on guard against attack from the Aboriginal tribes that were being displaced from their traditional land. It was very hard work moving forward with all their possessions and cattle! And when they arrived there were no houses waiting to be inhabited; just trees!

The early houses were known as 'slab huts,' because the roughly cut timber was placed in the ground in a vertical position. The roof was usually made of timber and corrugated iron - tin. Inside paper was often glued to the wooden slab walls in an effort to prevent the winds blowing into the home through the cracks. I have read of the people living in those homes, lying in bed and being able to see the stars through the cracks in the wall. Sometimes mice made their nests in the paper, and could be heard moving about between the slab wall and the paper.

Often the floors were paved with a mixture of sand and cattle manure, which set like cement for many months. When the floor began to break up it was everyone and everything outside while a new floor was mixed and laid.

In those days there were no churches, schools, doctors, telephone or cars. Usually the family, travelling by a horse drawn cart, visited a large town to buy supplies. They used bullock teams to convey their wool and wheat to the markets for sale. Others drove their stock to far away sale yards to be

auctioned to butchers. After a time in the town where the family bought supplies that would last for the next year, they set out on the long journey home.

Everyone in the family worked hard to build their homes, grow crops and take care of the sheep and cattle. In many places children grew up not being able to read or write because there were no schools. Their parents couldn't teach them as they had never attended school either!

How different this was from what we read in the Scriptures concerning God's people Israel, who were rescued from slavery in Egypt. The Lord raised up Moses to lead them to the Promised Land. God provided them with all they needed for the journey.

After Moses' death Joshua became their leader. God used the Israelites to overthrow the ungodly people who had settled on the land promised to Abraham and his descendants (Genesis 17: 8). Houses were ready to be occupied, crops were growing in the fields and cattle were waiting to be milked or killed for food. We can trust the words of our God when he said: 'A good man leaves an inheritance to his children's children, but the wealth of the sinner is stored up for the righteous' (Proverbs 13:22).

How different this was to the conditions faced by the men and women who settled in the outback regions of Australia - out beyond the *black stump*, and where the crows fly backwards to keep the dust out of their eyes.

What an adventure it would be to spend some time in the Australian outback.

Outback Cattle Stations

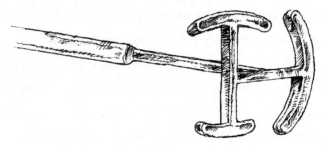

A ustralian outback land is less productive than the coastal region because of the low rainfall. This meant that the cattlemen needed huge tracts of land for their herds to graze in order to find sufficient food, with the result that Australia has some of the largest cattle stations in the world.

In the early days of white settlement in Australia, the cattle men drove their herds across the Great Dividing Range, onto the Western Plains and beyond where they selected land large enough for their stock. At first the boundary of each property was marked out by geographical features; for example the land between certain hills and on one side of a particular river. Later the property was surveyed so that the station owners knew the exact area of their property. The cattlemen then paid the government for the land they 'leased' which was usually for ninety-nine years.

In outback Queensland, Northern Territory and Western Australia there are cattle stations whose size is measured in square kilometres (or square miles). Some of them are more than 10,000 square kilometres (6,250 square miles) in size, with herds of cattle that number from 20,000 to over 80,000. There are some countries in Europe that are smaller in size than the Australian large cattle stations.

I read a story once. I don't know whether it is true or not, but it could well be so. The owner of a cattle station met a friend who had travelled by plane from England for a holiday. He was met by his cattleman mate who told him the drive to his homestead would take about ten hours. After a four hour drive the Australian said, "Well, we've reached our station."

When his friend asked, 'But where is your homestead?' the cattleman answered, 'We have just reached one boundary of our station. We have another six hours' drive before we come to the homestead!'

A Queensland family owns eleven cattle stations on which they run 130,000 head of cattle. A station in Northern Territory was once 25,000 square kilometres in size - a size that is difficult to imagine. Over the years portions were sold and the station is now somewhat smaller, just 16,000 square kilometres.

There is a constant need of water for the cattle, especially as in some places, rain might only fall a couple of times a year. Men will have to drill through the soil until they reach the artesian water. Sometimes the underground pressure forces the water to the surface. However, usually the pipe is connected to a windmill pump which brings the water into troughs for the animals to drink. There are not many windmills today as electric motors, powered by the sun's energy, are now used to pump up the water.

Years ago it was men and women on horseback who worked long hours caring for the cattle and rounding them up for the long drive to the sale yards. Over the years things have changed on the cattle station. Today workers often ride motor bikes with their cattle dog seated on the front between the cattleman's arms, ready to hop off and round up the herds at a moment's notice. The station manager frequently uses a helicopter to keep a watch over his property.

With abattoirs close to cattle stations the need to drive the cattle hundreds of miles to the sale yards is over. Today huge trucks of fifty metres length and divided into three or more sections are loaded with cattle for the sale yards or abattoirs. Some of these trucks have as many as 60 tyres. Carrying cattle this way means the animals arrive at their destination in good condition and in much faster time than droving.

The cattle and sheep stations are not fenced, as the cost would be astronomical. However fences are not needed to keep cattle on the station. Drinking water in strategic spots around the station ensures that the cattle do not stray too far away - they always remain within walking distance of the watering hole!

Water has always been important to farming communities. Just think how many stories there are in the Bible that mention wells and rivers. God provided water for his people in the middle of the desert on more than one occasion.

In Australia today most homesteads are modern homes. Electricity is provided from batteries charged with electricity from the sun. Water is pumped into high tanks that supply

the home with a water pressure
just like homes in the cities.
They have two-way
radios, equipment to
deal with accidents,
and radio or telephone
to contact the Flying
Doctor Service, the
School of the Air
or just to talk with
their friends many
kilometres away.

Today, most homesteads have satellite TV, and many other
modern conveniences.

However, the people living on the cattle stations miss out
on social activities and this applies particularly to the children
and women. The closest neighbour might be several hundred
kilometres away, and while the children and women talk to one
another on the radio they miss out on that personal contact.
The children usually have only a few other youngsters with
whom to play, but the men have their work mates to speak
with every day. The workers are usually a mixture of whites
and aboriginals, who enjoy one another's company. Mateship
is alive in the Australian outback!

The cattle are branded with a special sign marking
ownership. This is a rather cruel practice as the workers heat
the metal brand until it is glowing white hot and then burn
the owner's registered mark into the animal's skin near the hip.

I imagine that the burn is very painful for a couple of days, but the ownership mark is permanent.

As I was writing about the branding, I remembered that God chose a man called Abraham to be his friend. We read of the Lord's dealings with Abraham in Genesis, the first book of the Bible. Chapter 17 is an important chapter because it outlines the covenant (agreement) God made with him. Read that chapter and you will find that God required every baby boy who was descended from Abraham to carry a special mark in his body. He was circumcised, which the Lord said was to be 'a sign of the covenant between Me and you' (Genesis 17:11ff). Just as a brand on cattle marked out ownership, so circumcision marked the child as being a member of the Covenant people. Today it is baptism that marks out the person who is in a special relationship with God.

The Sheep Run

The Australian cattle and sheep stations are usually very big. Brunette Downs Station in Northern Territory is one of Australia's largest, being 1,221,296 hectares in area with a staff of thirty-five workers.

When the British settled in Australia they brought their precious animals with them. John MacArthur was an officer in charge of soldiers sent to guard the convicts. On his way to *The Land Down Under*, the ships called in to South Africa where they took on board fresh water and food. It was there that MacArthur purchased some merino sheep.

He and his wife, Elizabeth, devoted much time and energy to breeding sheep. The mutton was needed in the colony for food and the wool was sold to overseas merchants who in turn sold the wool to the factories that produced cloth. When John MacArthur was involved in an attempt to overthrow the colonial Governor, he was ordered to return to England and face charges. His wife Elizabeth had to look after the farm during his absence, and was largely responsible for cross breeding the sheep to produce better food and wool.

Soon after settlement it was discovered that the wet coastal area was not good for sheep as they suffered from foot rot. The rain made the wool very heavy and uncomfortable for the sheep, and the blow flies spoilt much wool when they infected the sheep. As a result the drovers and their families set out with their herds to claim properties in the outback. This meant crossing the Great Dividing Range which was hard work as there were no roadways. Families slept in tents or in wagons containing all their possessions. The boss, with his workers, usually slept in the open, under the stars.

As with the cattle stations, water was essential and the artesian bores provided the drinking water needed for the sheep. In some areas there are billabongs - large ponds of water sometimes found in the bed of a river, and streams that provide good drinking water. Water for humans came first from wherever it could be found, but soon tanks were collecting water that drained off the homestead roof.

Life on the sheep station was hard, especially for the women and children whose closest neighbours were many kilometres away. In the early years, the station owners, usually accompanied by their wives and children, took their bales of wool to the sales in large cities, and returned home with a year's supply of food and equipment. As many stations had a large quantity of wool it was necessary to transport it on large drays, pulled along by a bullock team or horses.

There is a lot to do on a sheep station. The animals have to be regularly dipped in troughs containing a poison to kill ticks and other pests. It is also necessary to keep the area about the sheep's tail free of infections, which if left, ruins the wool and endangers the health of the animal. Then there was the annual mustering and shearing of the flock.

There was and still is a big difference between the Australian and Biblical 'shepherds.' Most shepherds in the Scriptures were kind men who led their sheep and protected them from wild animals. Isaiah describes God as a kind shepherd: 'Behold, the Lord GOD shall come with a strong hand ... He will feed his flock like a shepherd; he will gather the lambs with his arm, and carry them in his bosom, and gently lead those who are with young' (Isaiah 40:10,11).

In Australia the stockman doesn't lead his sheep but rather rounds them up on horseback or a motor bike, making good use of his well-trained dogs.

Often you hear a sheep owner say that his dog is worth half a dozen men. A few shouts and a whistle and the dog is off to work, doing as he is told. When they are directed to go to the other side of the flock, they jump up on a sheep's back and cross the flock, jumping from sheep to sheep.

For many years dog trials have been held at major shows. The dogs and owners are judged on how well they work together as some sheep are rounded up and driven into small holding pens. These dogs are very clever!

Groups of shearers travel from shed to shed, shearing the sheep. It's hot, hard work, but the pay is good. The shearers and those who grade the wool are very important workers, as Australia produces some of the best wool in the world. Sometimes the men don't see their families for several months at a time, but when they return home they usually have a big pay packet.

There are times when a shearer will accidentally cut the sheep's skin. When this happens he calls for the young man who carries a tin of tar. With his small paint brush

he quickly applies the tar to the cut to stop the bleeding and prevent infection. It's all hard work in the shearing sheds and there are no air conditioners to make life comfortable. In recent years every effort is being made to make shearing easier. It is a great strain on the shearers' back as he spends most of the day bent over the sheep, but now in most sheds there is a rope hanging from the roof with a rubber loop on the end. The shearer adjusts the rope so that when the rubber is around his chest and stomach, it takes the weight off his legs.

Jesus said that he was the shepherd of his people. He is a gentle shepherd who cares for his people [sheep] in a more loving way than the Australian shepherd. He said, 'I am the good shepherd. The good shepherd gives his life for the sheep.... I am the good shepherd; and I know My sheep, and am known by my own. As the Father knows me, even so I know the Father; and I lay down my life for the sheep.

And other sheep I have which are not of this fold; them also I must bring, and they will hear my voice; and there will be one flock and one shepherd' (John 10:11-16).

Every Christian should know Psalm 23 - the Shepherd's Psalm. Please make sure that you know it: ' The LORD is my shepherd; I shall not want. He makes me to lie down in green pastures; he leads me beside the still waters. He restores my soul; he leads me in the paths of righteousness for his name's sake. Yea, though I walk through the valley of the shadow of death, I will fear no evil; For you are with me; your rod and your staff, they comfort me. You prepare a table before me in the presence of my enemies; you anoint my head with oil; my cup runs over. Surely goodness and mercy shall follow me all the days of my life; And I will dwell in the house of the LORD Forever.'

May the Lord Jesus be your shepherd to guide you through life's journey, along that narrow way, and bring you to that great destination - heaven!

The Rabbit-proof fence

There must be millions of miles of fencing throughout the world, and each of those fences serves a special purpose. Many fences in the city are there to decorate the homes that have been built.

In some towns and cities fences mark out land ownership, and prevent undesirable people coming in. The same fence is important to make sure children are safe, and the dog is kept in. In many Australian backyards there is a swimming pool. About 40 children drown in those pools each year and in an effort to prevent this happening the government has made the construction of a fence around the pool compulsory.

In country areas, and this includes the outback areas of Australia, homes are fenced to guard the lawn, flowers and vegetables from animals. Cattle are kept on their own property, while the neighbour's animals are prevented from getting in and eating the precious crops.

In outback Australia the sheep and cattle stations are huge and in most cases the only fence to be seen is the one around the homestead and another about the mustering paddock.

Now some of you who are reading this book may have a lovely, furry rabbit as a pet. There were no rabbits in the 'Land Down Under' before the white settlers arrived. The Aboriginal children certainly didn't have any pet rabbits; they would have had a pet dingo or some other native animal. However, our early white settlers brought rabbits with them. Possibly some were brought for food while others were the family pet. The little animals are furry and lovely to cuddle, but they eat grass, lettuce, carrots and many other vegetables. Consequently they are not liked by landowners because of the damage they do to the land and crops. Soon after the settlement in Australia by the British, rabbits escaped and within a few years the settlers noticed many rabbits on their properties eating the food that was being grown for cattle and humans - rabbits then became noxious pests!

The scientists tell us that ten rabbits can eat as much pasture in a day as does one sheep. The rabbit population grew at a rapid rate and soon the cattle and sheep stations were feeding millions of those lovely little animals, which meant the land could no longer support as many sheep and beef cattle as before. In many areas they eat every blade of grass, leaving the soil unprotected in times of strong winds and flood. There have been times when the strong inland winds have blown the inland dust, not just to the ocean, but across the Tasman Sea to New Zealand. I would like to tell you something here about those duststorms where the wind blows fiercely and the valuable topsoil becomes airborne. Those living in houses set to work at once in an effort to stop the fine dust getting over everything. Every crack is blocked up, but usually a fine layer of dust settles on everything. The rabbits are partly to blame for the loss of the topsoil.

Not only do the rabbits eat the grass, and crops, but they ring-bark trees - they chew the life-giving layer between the bark and the wood, killing trees. Graziers have done all they can to control the rabbit plague - they have ploughed in their burrows, shot and poisoned the pests, but their numbers continued to grow.

Then the Governments stepped in and decided to build rabbit proof fences to keep the rabbits from spreading all over Australia.

In 1896 the Governments of South Australia and Western Australia decided to build this fence. The first post hole was dug in December, 1901 and for seven years, gangs of men dug post holes and trenches between the posts for the wire netting fence. The netting had to go deep into the ground to prevent the rabbits digging their way under.

Instead of just one fence, those pesky rabbits kept moving ahead of the men doing the fencing. This meant that a second and a third fence had to be built. By 1908 three fences had been erected, more than 3 000 miles in length.

Keeping the fence repaired proved difficult. There was little food for the horses and camels that were first used to transport men and equipment. When the repair gangs began to use trucks the rough, stony ground easily punctured the tyres. It was very hard, hot work for the men who spent their time keeping the rabbit proof fence in a state of good repair.

There is no doubt that in some areas these fences have done a good job. On one side where the rabbits have eaten all pastures up to the fence, the land is bare. On the other side the land is still green with grass. That of course was what was originally intended.

There have been several attempts to eradicate rabbits by introducing myxomatosis which killed millions, but before long they became immune to the virus. Killing rabbits this way is very cruel. I have seen some who were almost blind, unable to find food and were very sick.

For many years a company not far from where we live has been manufacturing hats used by farmers and stockmen. They use the fur of about nine rabbits to make one hat, which encouraged people to trap rabbits - but the rabbit population continues to explode.

Today we find some men farming rabbits for food. Of course they are enclosed by rabbit proof fences that prevent any escapes.

In my Bible the word 'fence' appears only once, and that is in Psalm 62:3. In that age fences were often 'walls' and that word appears 69 times and the word 'wall' is there 176 times.

In the days of the Old Testament, walls were built for the

same reason that we build a fence today. One wall spoken of in the New Testament, is in the book of 'Revelation.' This fence is used to divide one group of people from another group. Do you know it?

Revelation 21:9-27 describes the wall about the great city called 'the holy Jerusalem' (Revelation 21:10). We are told that certain people will have permission to enter through the gates and into God's city: 'Blessed are those who do his commandments, that they may have the right to the tree of life, and may enter through the gates into the city' (Rev 22:14). God's people are those who are born again. They love God and are saved by the Lord Jesus Christ. They are citizens of the Kingdom of Heaven.

Outside we are told are 'dogs and sorcerers and sexually immoral and murderers and idolators, and whoever loves and practises a lie' (Rev 22:15). Every person who has no interest in the Lord Jesus Christ is a citizen of Satan's kingdom and will never find a home for himself in Christ's kingdom, unless God changes them.

In the Australian outback, the rabbit proof fence didn't control the movements of all the rabbits. Some dug under the wire netting fence and others simply hopped through gaping holes where cattle and kangaroos had knocked the fence down. They ate bare the pastures which were for the cattle; but rest assured that God's wall will keep out every person who is not a Christian.

On which side of God's wall are you standing today?

Wheat

The outback regions of Australia are usually rather dry, and bores must be sunk to get the underground water for the stock. While this water is not pure, the cattle drink it and survive - and put on weight when there is food for them to eat. However, it is not just sheep and cattle that do well in the outback. Wheat is grown in abundance; so much in fact that Australia is the world's eighth largest wheat producer and the fifth largest exporter of that precious seed. Depending upon the season, Australia's forty thousand wheat producers annually export about twenty million tonnes to needy countries.

When white people settled in 'The Land Down Under' they planted wheat along the coast, but the high rainfall caused the disease called rust, to spoil the crop. The first person to grow wheat in the colony was the Rev Richard Johnson, but it is James Ruse who is best known for his small wheat production. Just south of Sydney at Campbelltown you will find his tombstone on which is chiselled his claim to be the first in Sydney to grow wheat. Ruse was a convict who was born in Cornwall, England in 1760. He was transported to Australia in the 1st fleet in 1788 because he had broken into a house in 1782. He was granted his freedom in 1789 and asked for a piece of land as he had decided to make Australia his home. His farm was very small, about half a hectare in size with a small hut on it. He married Elizabeth Perry in 1790, the same year in which he planted wheat and maize.

While he did not grow the first wheat, he produced sufficient wheat seed to use in his home for twelve months, enough to plant his next crop and with some left over to sell. He proved that it was possible for anyone who was willing to work, to support himself without receiving government help. His wheat however suffered from *rust*, which showed him that wheat had to be grown in a drier climate.

Soon settlers began to move over the Blue Mountains to commence wheat farming in the Australian inland regions which received less rain. Here there is usually some rainfall at planting time. In normal seasons there is sufficient rain to produce a good crop. Harvesting takes place when there is no rain to spoil the seed. Growing wheat in the inland regions of our continent meant that roads and railways had to be constructed to transport the crop to the coastal city ports where much was shipped overseas. The big mills that produce flour for the Australian market are to be found in the coastal cities.

In those early days of inland settlement, wheat farming was difficult because there were only horses to drag the plough, the harrow and the harvester. The plough turned over the soil, but was continually being snagged on large rocks or tree stumps. This meant that the person doing the work had to stop and waste precious time releasing the equipment. It wasn't long before 'The Stump Jump Plough' was invented. When this plough struck some tree roots or large rocks it 'jumped' over the obstruction saving the farmer valuable time disengaging it from the obstacle. After ploughing, the soil was broken up using the harrow. This meant that anything growing on the land enriched the soil. It also allowed the rain to soak well down into the ground to assist the early growth of the crop. Many years ago the farm workers had to walk along in a cloud of dust behind the farm implements that were pulled along by a large number of big draught horses.

Today these horses are rarely seen; in fact the only time they are seen is at shows. They are used in ploughing competitions where the winner is the man and horse that ploughs the straightest furrow.

Life on the farm was hard and every member of the family was expected to do their part in making sure a good crop was harvested. Many farmers kept their children away from school as they were needed to work the land. How would you like this to happen to you? In those days attendance at school was not compulsory and many children grew up unable to read and write. Towards the end of the 19th century school attendance was made compulsory and free. The law today is the same - compulsory, free education for all children from six to fifteen or sixteen years. It is because of this law that most Australian children can read and write. Reading is a great skill that makes it possible for you to read  your Bible.

Gradually farm implements became more efficient, and when the petrol engine was invented wide ploughs, harrows, and harvesters were used to produce huge crops of wheat. Today, wheat paddocks are immense, with some well over two hundred hectares. The wheat is stored in silos that are built in the wheat producing areas. Trains with many carriages then transport the seed to the large coastal cities where it is milled for local consumption and sale overseas.

Farm working conditions have improved greatly. Now the men driving the machines sit in comfortable, air-conditioned cabins listening to the radio. Many have phones so drivers can get help when it is needed. All the men working in the open wear a mask as the air is full of dust.

In my Bible I find wheat mentioned many times - 49 times my computer tells me. Wheat has always been a very important food. Today, wheat flour is used to make bread, cakes, biscuits, breakfast cereals, pancakes and many other tasty foods.

There were times when Christians were called *wheat*. John the Baptist said of Jesus: 'He will baptise you with the Holy

Spirit and fire.... and he will thoroughly clean out his threshing floor, and gather the *wheat* into his barn ...' (Luke 3:15,17). All of you who have trusted the Lord for your salvation are like those precious wheat seeds. It is true that the death of Christ saved many sinners; so many that we could not count them (John 12:24; Revelation 7:9,10).

Jesus told his disciples that the world contained people who belonged to him. Christians have the task of bringing in the harvest - bringing sinners to their Saviour. There is so much work to be done and so few labourers. The Saviour said: 'The harvest truly is plentiful, but the labourers are few. Therefore pray the Lord of the harvest to send out labourers into his harvest' (Matthew 9:37-38). We are called to be 'harvesters' to tell people of Christ. We must leave it to the Holy Spirit to bring about the new birth and membership in the Kingdom of God.

Today it is a wonderful sight to look over the fields with the golden heads of wheat swaying like waves in the ocean. Every time you take some bread or cake in your hand ask yourself whether you have been 'harvested' by one of the Lord's labourers. If you are a Christian, you are one of Christ's reapers and have work to do, telling others about the gospel.

Get on with that important work!

Big Red

Tourists expect to see kangaroos on the streets of Sydney. This is not so! Gradually most of the kangaroos on the coastal plain have been driven inland because of the spread of population and intensive farming along the coastal regions of the nation.

Many years ago you would hear children singing the theme song of the TV show for children - 'Skippy.':

'Skippy, Skippy, Skippy the bush kangaroo.'

Skippy was a small grey roo that was once found along the eastern coastal plains. In earlier days some people had kangaroos as pets, but today it is illegal to have one locked up in the backyard. It is likely that some of the children living in the outback have a kangaroo, wallaby, or a joey [a baby kangaroo] which they call their pet.

In Australia there are over 60 different species of kangaroos, but I would like to write something about the true outback ones where the male is known as 'Big Red' or 'Old Man Red.' These animals are the biggest of their species and get their nickname because of the reddish fur of the male.

They are found in regions where there is only a small annual rainfall. The 'Big Red' is found on the Australian Coat of Arms. He can only move forward! Do you remember what they depict? It depicts Australia's forward movement in both national and world affairs. Unfortunately it doesn't represent the growth of Christianity in Australia. The male roo can grow up to 1.8 metres in height and weigh 90 kg; and the smoky-blue female, the 'Blue Flier' can stand 1.25 metres in height and weigh up to 35 kg.

God gave these animals the teeth they would need to graze on grass. Driving along the roadway during the heat you will see many kangaroos lying down in the shade of the trees because it is too hot in the middle of the day for eating. In the early morning and late afternoon they spend time grazing on the grasses, and sometimes eating any fungi they find. When night falls they again settle down to a night's rest. Some of the mobs contain as many as 100 animals. They do not wander more than ten or twenty kilometres from a water supply.

The mobs are really groups of individual families, living together where there is food and water. Living close together means they do socialise a lot with one another. Often one will approach a member of another family and for a time will sniff one another and touch noses and lips. Sometimes they will even groom each other. When one animal asserts his superiority, usually through fighting, the defeated one will bow to the ground with a quivering head. There are occasions when there is serious fighting to prove a male's superiority. The animals grab one another about the neck with their strong forepaws and leaning back on their powerful tail use one foot and toe to rip the skin off their opponent. Sometimes the blow can be fatal!

Kangaroos are food to many aboriginal tribes. Warrigals, known as dingoes or native dogs, are an enemy of the roo, but frequently the kangaroo comes off the victor. They grab the dingo in their strong short arms and tear open the flesh, killing or severely injuring the attacker. Sometimes the roo will escape from a Warrigal, by jumping into a stream or river. When the native dog comes after him the roo will grab his enemy and hold it under the water until it drowns.

Like children, joeys enjoy playing together. They also teach one another the art of fighting. They stand face to face and with their forepaws touch one another as if they were about to commence a boxing match. They grab their opponent gently about the neck and kick with their strong back legs.

The kangaroo is a marsupial - it carries its young in its pouch. When the baby is about 30 to 40 days old it is born

and commences its first journey up the front of the mother, and into her pouch where it attaches itself to a nipple for about one hundred and twenty five days. At this stage in life the hairless, blind, tiny joey weighs only about one quarter of an ounce. When it is about six months old the joey begins to leave its mother's pouch and explore the world.

This is an example of the wonderful natural life of Australia and an example of God's marvellous creation. They give us a glimpse of God's wonderful creativity and power.

Joeys keep close to their mothers and dive into the pouch when life is dangerous. If there is danger the mother roo bounds away with the joey in her pouch. Frequently the mother will hide her joey in a clump of bushes and bound away to lead the dogs away from the young roo.

When we are in danger from sin and are tempted to disobey God we should ask him for help and protection. We need safety and security from God. In Psalm 46:1 we read, 'My God is an ever-present help in trouble.' In Romans 8:26 we are told that the Holy Spirit helps us in our weakness. So when we face temptation, trouble and other difficulties God will provide help. We just need to ask him. In Psalm 18:6 it says 'I cried to my God for help.' We should do this too.

While the joey drinks from its mother she grooms her baby. The pouch is a place of security for him and often the mother roo can be seen grazing with a joey's leg protruding from the pouch.

In times of drought they become pests to the sheep and cattle men as they eat the grass needed by stock. They find themselves attacked by dingoes, foxes, eagles and humans. There are times, when, owing to big increases in their numbers, the Government gives permission for the animals to be culled. Many end up as food for pets. Floods and cold weather cause the death of many. Despite this, the kangaroo population is high. In 1999 it was estimated that there were 29.9 million Red, Western Grey and Eastern Grey roos. The total kangaroo population in Australia is estimated to be more than 50 million.

While grazing, kangaroos shuffle along, but will move quickly if in danger. The Old Man Red hops along at 25 kilometres/hour without using too much energy. When greater speed is needed the hopping rate remains about the same although the length of each hop increases. The Western Red is able to speed along at 70 kilometresm/hr for a short period of time.

Today kangaroo meat is eaten in Australia and overseas. The meat is high in protein and low in fat. The skin is strong and is often used to make sporting footwear. The Kangaroo industry is closely monitored by the Government. The export of live kangaroos is prohibited, except in the case of zoos.

A kangaroo is a strange animal. They are very small when born and grow to a good height. They can hop along very quickly. When we see in creation the great variety of animals, birds and fish it is impossible to understand the mind of God who created all things. The world about us is wonderful, despite the effects of sin. When you spend time in the countryside have a close look at God's handiwork and praise him for all that he has done.

Big bird

In this chapter you will learn something about the bird, that with the kangaroo, is found on the Australian Coat of Arms. It is the emu; a bird that cannot run backwards. This says that Australia is always on the march forward.

A lot of countries have big birds, but in Australia we have the second biggest bird in the world - the emu. There are many unusual things about the emu that we don't find in other birds. The first is that it cannot fly. Even the emu's name is strange. This is not a word from the English language, nor from the languages of the Australian aboriginal, the 'Koori' people, but is an Arabic word meaning 'a large bird'. The fully grown emu is rather large. If you stood in front of a mature one, you would be facing a bird about 1.9 metres tall. He is so tall that he can look down on most people and you would have to look upwards to see his eye! Fully grown he can weigh up to 45 kg.

It has grey, brown feathers with small wings and long, strong legs. Each foot has three toes pointing forward.

They are usually seen in groups searching for food, but they are not very sociable birds. A long time ago emus were found on the coastal plains, but the spread of population and destruction of their habitat has driven them inland. They are no longer seen in numbers except in the outback. Many years ago they were found in Tasmania, Kangaroo Island and King Island, but they were exterminated by the white settlers.

Today the estimated emu population of Australia numbers about one million. They eat plants, insects, plant roots, seeds, fruit, insects, droppings and small animals. Like most birds they eat small stones that help grind up the food they have eaten. When food becomes scarce they move on to find better pastures. They have been known to move over one hundred kilometres searching for a food supply; some groups are known to move up to twenty five kilometres in a day.

They make a loud booming noise, using an air sack in their neck. This pouch is about 30 cm long in the adult bird and the sound can be heard up to two kilometres away. In their groupings the adults make grunting sounds while the chickens make a high pitched whistle.

Their breeding habits are different to almost every other creature in the world, including humans. Many years ago most families had a mother who stayed home and cared for the house and children. It was Dad who went out and worked to earn a living. However, we should never fall into the trap of thinking that mothers who stay home do not work. They are responsible for caring for the family which involves a lot of work. If you have the time, read what the Bible says in Proverbs 31:10-31 about the godly woman.

Today both parents usually work in order to provide food,

clothing and a home for the family. In some situations it is Mum who earns a living and Dad who stays home to look after the house and children.

The emu family is very unusual. After mating both mother and father build a nest on the ground. Grass and leaves are stacked together until the hatchery is about 10 cm high and 2 metres in diametre. Then the female lays as many as 10 eggs, each about 130 mm by 90 mm, each coloured a dark blue and green. If they are left too long in the sun, their colour is bleached.

At this point in the nesting process, the male emu starts hunting all emus away from what he believes to be his nest. He even hunts away the emu mother who laid the eggs. It is then the responsibility of the male to care for the eggs, and the chickens. He sits faithfully on the nest for about 55 days until the eggs hatch. During that time he makes sure no egg

drinks no water and does not leave the nest at any time. That is hard to believe isn't it? However, it's true!

When the eggs hatch the chicks commence eating at once and stay with their father for up to six months. The chickens have black or brown stripes along their body. They in turn breed when they are about 20 months old.

In the meantime the mother emu usually finds another mate and again lays eggs for a second family. Again the male will hunt her away while he cares for the eggs and later the chicks.

Life for the emu can be very dangerous. Besides humans who killed many, the Tasmanian Tiger, now extinct, played its part in killing the entire population of emus in Tasmania and the adjacent islands. Their source of food and water is being destroyed by buildings and farming practices. They can exist in the cold southern regions of Australia and in the hot wet regions in the far north, but mainly they live in the inland. Dingoes run them down and kill many, while eagles play their part killing big numbers. When they are being chased by

an eagle they run in a zig-zag pattern which helps them escape. They can get away from the dingo by jumping into deep water - a creek, billabong or river where they can swim away. They are capable of running at a speed of 50 kilometres per hour taking strides three metres in length. When cornered they turn and fight, lashing out with their long, strong legs and sharp claws. Many dingoes have come to grief with injuries caused this way.

In Australia now, many people have started farming the emu as the returns are good. A bird can provide 75 kilograms of good meat which has little fat or cholesterol. The two square metres of leather from each bird has many uses but much is used to make shoes as it is so strong. The feathers weighing 2.75 kilograms are used for decorative work, while the 1.5 litres of oil has proved useful in treating our aches and pains. On infertile, hollow eggs skilled artists have painted scenes which have proved very popular with tourists. Some very gifted people engrave scenes on egg shells which are also sold.

Emus are not mentioned in the Scriptures, but they are part of God's creation, and we can learn something from the character of the bird. The male cares for his offspring for many months and teaches them the way to live. We should not be like him and drive one parent away. Sadly in our world many families consist of just one parent, and in other families both mother and family are absent. Regardless of these sad situations the head of the family has important responsibilities. We read in 1 Timothy 5:8 a serious warning: 'But if anyone does not provide for his own, and especially for those of his household, he has denied the faith and is worse than an unbeliever.'

The head of the household has the responsibility for teaching the young people about the Lord Jesus Christ and the truth of the Scriptures. In Deuteronomy 6:5-9 we read: 'You shall love the LORD your God with all your heart, with all your soul, and with all your strength. And these words which I command you today shall be in your heart. You shall teach them diligently to your children, and shall talk of them when you sit in your house, when you walk by the way, when you lie down, and when you rise up. You shall bind them as a sign on your hand, and they shall be as frontlets between your eyes. You shall write them on the doorposts of your house and on your gates.'

The Apostle Paul also reminded the head of the household to do the same. We read: 'And you, fathers, do not provoke your children to wrath, but bring them up in the training and admonition of the Lord' (Ephesians 6:4).

I trust that you will listen carefully to what you are taught by mums, dads, grandmas, grandfathers, minister and Sunday School teacher while you are growing up, and that you appreciate all the care and attention they have given you.

Australian Aborigines

It is believed that the first Aboriginal people arrived on Australian soil many years ago. They made their way by boat to their new home. This meant they travelled from a country to the north of Australia, moving from island to island across the open sea. Having arrived, they established tribal boundaries, living off the food that was found close-by. Some also sailed across Bass Strait to make their home in Tasmania. From the time the Kooris settled this land until the British settlement in 1788, some 600 tribes were formed having a population of about 300,000.

Those who settled along the coast found plenty of food which made life easy. Those who moved to the Australian outback found life to be very difficult due to the lack of consistent rain, but they found places where there was fresh water and always carefully covered it over to prevent evaporation. Having become skilful hunters they lived off the local food supply. Kangaroos, wallabies, lizards and a multitude of smaller animals were killed and eaten. Often the bush was set alight to drive the animals out, where they were speared and killed for food. Where there was water in billabongs, rivers and creeks, fish and water birds could be easily caught. This gave them a variety of foods for their meals. Other birds were also killed and eaten, especially the emu.

However there was no electricity to run refrigerators, which meant food had to be caught almost on a daily basis. The men were excellent hunters and their skill was important to keep the family alive. The Kooris crept up on their prey by covering their bodies with mud and holding the branch of a tree in front of themselves. When they were close enough they would throw their spear or boomerang with great accuracy. Catching water birds was simple. With a hollow twig allowing them to breathe underwater they slowly moved towards the birds. Then, without showing themselves, they would grab

the legs and pull the bird underwater before it could make a sound. The women searched for honey, witchetty grubs, snakes, lizards, edible seeds, plants and yams.

The Kooris didn't have the things we take for granted. There were no horses, cattle, roads, books, schools, doctors or a common language - and much more. There were no matches to light a fire. This was done by rubbing two sticks together. The wheel had not been invented and axes were made from sharpened stone, bound to a wooden handle. The children were taught the skills they would need later in life. Small related groups were members of the 'clan'. Clans spoke the same language, had a common religion and intermarried.

When Captain Cook sailed along the Australian coast in 1770 he saw some of the natives. He wrote in his log that they

looked like 'the most wretched [people] upon the earth.' He went on to say they appeared to be living a very contented life and were much happier than the Europeans.

The Kooris worshipped their own gods and rock art found in caves shows the people dancing around the god that was worshipped. Those taking part in the dancing (Corroboree) painted their bodies. Art work was also carved on flat wood. Some of their religious stories were told in secret only to those who would become tribal members. Some stories and dancing belonged to the men alone while women had their secret ceremonies.

You will read in another chapter about Ayers Rock found in the Australian outback. The name of this large rock is now Uluru. This region features heavily in the aboriginal stories. These stories are referred to as the *Dreamtime* stories. The Kooris invented stories about Red Lizards who threw boomerangs and creatures called Bell-Bird men and Lizard men

Wherever the Kooris lived they had their own peculiar myths which were handed down in stories and paintings. The clan traced over the paintings to ensure they lasted to all generations.

When someone behaved in a way that harmed the tribal members the medicine man could with great ceremony point the bone at the accused person. So strong was the belief that pointing the bone caused death of the person at whom the bone was pointed, he went away and soon after died. We should be thankful that we have access to the truth of God and access to God himself through his Son Jesus Christ. It is the truth that sets us free - free from fear and sin and death. God's Word, the Bible, tells amazing stories that are true and not human inventions.

Aboriginal children accepted the customs and teaching of their elders. Mothers-to-be talked to their babies even while in the womb. If you know of people who have told you about the Lord Jesus Christ since you were a baby you should thank God for them. Pray to God that he will help you to become one of those people who go out into the whole world to spread the truth about Jesus Christ and the good news of how God has come to save us.

Outback Kooris lived in homes (gunyahs) made of tree branches and bark. Those who lived in an area of rocks and hills could make a more substantial dwelling, but the natives were nomadic, ever moving onwards, always knowing where it was possible to find water, in holes, or soaks and from certain trees. When times were hard they dug up a variety of frogs that stored water in their bodies, and squeezed them very hard!

With the British settlement of Australia the Kooris found their way of life greatly disturbed. Any animal that crossed their tribal land could be killed for food, but when the sheep and cattlemen discovered that the natives were killing their stock, they took action. Many natives were murdered by the whites who believed they were a far superior race and the aboriginals little more than animals. In 1788 it was estimated that 1,500 natives lived in the Sydney area. Sixty years later there was just one! Today [A.D. 2004] there are quite a few living there!

Many died from what we consider to be minor illnesses - measles, chickenpox, tuberculosis, mumps and the flu. And the Kooris were supplied with alcohol that destroyed their self image. The natives' close attachment to their land was not considered important by the white settlers who believed land was property to be bought and sold.

The treatment of the Kooris by the white settlers often resulted in warfare, but the battle was so uneven that the natives were in the end utterly defeated. In 1824 martial law was proclaimed at a small country town called Bathurst. The natives had killed seven whites. The attack that followed by the police, settlers and soldiers resulted in the deaths of as many as one hundred natives.

An unusual event that took place in 1867/ 1868 was the visit of a Koori cricket team to Great Britain. One member of the team died and others were sent home because of the cold climate.

Today in Australia there is a move to correct some of the injustices that happened in the early days of settlement and afterwards. In some areas land is being returned to its rightful Koori owners who are providing work for their own people.

Children were forcibly removed from their parents to be taught the *superior* European way of life. Some were taken from their parents to be cared for by churches on reserves set aside for that purpose. Others found themselves living in homes of the white settlers where they were taught the ways of 'the white men.' Many were unjustly treated, but a few speak out and say that it was in the homes of kindly Christian people they came to know Christ as their Lord and Saviour.

The story of the Australian Koori people is a sad one. They lost their land to the British who took it by force. Many died from sickness brought to Australia by the migrants. The Christian Churches largely failed in their Christian duty of providing help and protection for the conquered people.

Efforts are being made by the AIM - the Australian Indigenous Ministry - and others to take the gospel to the Koori people. Native men are being trained to take up the work of preaching Christ and so fulfilling the command of the Lord himself: 'All authority has been given to me in heaven and on earth. Go therefore and make disciples of all the nations, baptising them in the name of the Father and of the Son and of the Holy Spirit, teaching them to observe all things that I have commanded you; and lo, I am with you always, even to the end of the age.' Amen' (Matthew 28: 18- 20).

Christians everywhere have the responsibility of taking the gospel to sinners. Have you ever told someone about the saving work of the Lord Jesus? Christians in the past have failed in their Christian duty - we should not let this happen again.

The Flying Doctor

Many years ago one of the greatest difficulties faced by people living in the Australian outback was caring for the sick and injured. Sit and think for a couple of minutes about this situation - You live on an outback cattle station and start to have pains in your stomach which your mum and dad think is being caused by your appendix which urgently needs removing. Your parents know that you need medical help immediately, but there is no doctor who can come to you. The closest lives 200 kilometres away. Is Dad to sharpen his rabbit skinning knife, cut open your stomach and remove what he thinks is your appendix, while Mum and some of the workers hold you down?

Or maybe you have tooth ache! Would Dad take out his greasy pliers and pull out your tooth while you were tied to a chair screaming and kicking?

Accidents often happen to people living in very isolated places, hundreds of kilometres from the nearest town and doctor. Just one story shows the need of urgent medical help in the outback. This is a true story of a stockman by the name of Jimmy Darcy who was severely injured in a fall from his horse. It was August, 1917, and Jimmy's mates took him to Halls Creek, a journey of 50 miles. Because of the serious nature of his injuries he could only be moved with great care, and the trip took 12 hours. As there was no doctor or nurse living and working at outback Halls Creek, the postman tried to contact a doctor living at Wyndham or Derby using morse code on the telegraph. He was probably the only person present who knew the Morse code alphabet!

When this failed he telegraphed a Perth doctor, whose first-aid lectures he had attended years before. Perth is about three thousand kilometres from Halls Creek. A conversation took place using morse code, in which the doctor told the postman what he was to do to the stockman. The stockman had injured his bladder and for two hours, using his well sharpened pocket knife, the post master did as the doctor instructed. As soon as possible the doctor, weighed down with his medical equipment, set out on the journey from Perth to Halls Creek, travelling by boat, in a T model Ford, on horseback and the final section of the trip on foot. Sad to say, the stockman died the day before the doctor arrived. His death was the result of both infections in the wound and from malaria.

Three things contributed to the safety of people living in outback Australia. The first was the radio. Morse code was superseded by voice, which meant those living in isolated regions were kept up-to-date with world events; but of greater

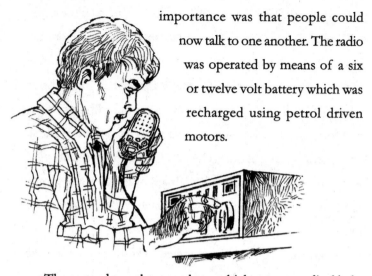

importance was that people could now talk to one another. The radio was operated by means of a six or twelve volt battery which was recharged using petrol driven motors.

The second was the aeroplane, which meant medical help could quickly be sent to an outback station, and patients flown to a city hospital. Virtually every cattle station, sheep run and country town soon had a runway. Some airstrips on the outback stations were rough and the plane bounced about as it landed and took off. If the doctor was needed during the night in those early days, the aerodrome was marked out with kerosene lamps. At other times a couple of cars or tractors, with their lights turned on, marked out the level ground. Landing and taking off was risky because of the state of the landing areas, but also because of animals - emus and kangaroos frequently wandered about the landing site.

The third thing to improve safety was the great advances in medicine, which meant the doctor on the plane had with him the most up-to-date equipment and medicines available. Patients in the outback could now receive medical treatment almost equal to that of their city cousins.

Today every person living in the outback feels much safer, because of the *Royal Flying Doctor Service*. The Reverend John Flynn, a Christian minister of the Presbyterian Church, is regarded as the man responsible for this great medical scheme. Flynn had been contacted by a young man, Lieutenant Clifford Peel, urging him to develop this proposal, suggesting that missionary doctors, be appointed to the outback. Sadly, the young man was killed during the First World War, but others saw the need and came to Flynn's help.

In 1912 John Flynn was appointed Superintendent of the Australian Inland Mission (AIM), which meant he was responsible for the spiritual well being of outback Presbyterians in an area of 300,000 sq kilometres in Western Australia and 1,500,00 sq kilometres in the Northern Territory. At that time there were only two doctors responsible for the medical care of people living in those isolated places. Flynn set about overcoming the need of these people to have immediate access to the best medical treatment possible.

At first he established small bush hospitals where a nurse was ready to give help when needed, but he and others began discussing his proposal for a flying doctor, and calling for donations to get the service established. In 1928 the AIM had sufficient money to start the Flying Doctor Service in outback Australia. Some wealthy people and managers of big industries came to the aid of Flynn's scheme. McKay, whose company manufactured the Sunshine Harvester, a machine for harvesting wheat, gave support, as did Hudson Fysh of QANTAS - Australia's first airline.

In May, 1928, it was decided to give the scheme a one year trial which was a resounding success. From that time onwards, the Flying Doctor Service made life in the outback much safer. The first plane was hired from QANTAS. It was a biplane having just one engine. The body of the plane was covered with a stiff canvas-like material and it cruised along at about one hundred and thirty kilometres per hour. In addition to the pilot there was space for four seated passengers.

But who was John Flynn, often referred to as 'Flynn of the Inland.'? He was born in a year that many Australians might remember for another reason - 1880 - the year in which the bushranger, Ned Kelly was hanged. John's father was a school teacher, but when his mother died he was cared for by relatives. Some years later the family was reunited at Snake Gully, not far from the gold mining region of Ballarat.

When the family was transferred to Melbourne, John commenced his study for the ministry. He became a graduate of Melbourne University and was ordained in 1911. When appointed to the AIM, he became one of a group of Pastors who, using horses and camels, travelled through the lonely outback regions of Australia. Because of his report to the Synod of the Presbyterian Church in 1912, he was appointed as head of the newly established AIM.

John Flynn died in 1952 and was buried near Alice Springs, at a place called Mt Gillen, which was roughly the centre of the great outback regions, whose people he had helped, both spiritually and medically. John Flynn was a great Australian Christian.

On the Australian $20 note, there is a picture of John Flynn and one of the planes used in the early days of the Flying Doctor Service. Today this service is responsible for the health of people living in the vast interior regions of Australia. It is supported by gifts and regular funding by the State and Federal Governments.

Now the Flying Doctor makes regular trips with dentists, doctors, specialists and nurses. These specialists give regular medical checkups to people living out there beyond the 'black stump.' There is no doubt that the Australian outback is a much safer place because of the work of John Flynn.

Now doctors are ready to come at once when needed. Parents don't have to be over-concerned when requiring medical help for their children and station workers. No longer do people depend upon radio to call The Flying Doctor Service as telephones are now used. Every outback station is equipped with a medical chest containing drugs, bandages and other medical equipment all in numbered packages. The contents of every medical chest is numbered the same so no mistakes can be made in carrying out the doctor's orders. The box has a picture of the various parts of the human body, which is used to diagnose complaints. Often it is not necessary for the doctor to travel great distances to see the patient, but he simply tells the person on the phone what is to be used by giving the number printed on the drugs in the medicine cabinet.

There are many stories about the treatments ordered by the doctor on duty. One man whose wife became very ill, was told by the doctor to give his wife a tablet from package number seven. Later he rang the doctor to tell him his wife was well on the way to a full recovery: 'We didn't have any of number seven left so I gave her one of number four and one of number three. She very quickly recovered.' At least the man could count!

Flynn's work reminds me of the Lord Jesus, who went about teaching that 'the Kingdom of God [was] at hand' (Mark 1:15). This was the work of John Flynn and all Christian ministers. They preach that the Kingdom of God can only be entered through the new birth which gives a sinner a saving faith in the Lord Jesus. Like our Saviour, the Flying Doctor brings both physical and spiritual healing to the hurt bodies and minds of people living way out where the crows fly backwards.

Jesus carried the sins of his people to the cross, and died in their place. Because of a perfect life of obedience to his heavenly Father, he gave his righteousness to his people, making it possible for them to be members of the Kingdom of Heaven. When the Lord Jesus walked this earth he performed great healing miracles. Today he has the same power as he did then.

We have a wonderful Saviour. Let us all imitate him by living a godly life and doing all we can for the well-being of others - both spiritually and physically.

Radio School

What's school like for you? I can still remember some of my school days at a small three teacher school. I had a lot of friends and thoroughly enjoyed the games we played, the sporting competitions and the annual athletics carnival. I was the champion marble player! I loved reading, writing stories, poetry ... in fact I enjoyed all of my subjects except art; I'm no artist! When I could read I discovered a new world with every new book. My brother and I rode our bicycles to school - about five kilometres distant. We grew up on a coastal farm and our closest friends lived about a kilometre away.

Now try and imagine living in outback Australia where the closest neighbour lives at least fifty kilometres away. To get there you would have to ride a horse across some desert region where there was no water for you or your horse.

Of course there might be a couple of families living near the station homestead and you would have several friends. But what about education? When Australia was first settled education was not compulsory, and those people who moved inland had no schools. It depended upon parents to educate their children. Those living way out beyond 'the black stump' had no opportunity to receive an education, except where a governess was employed to care for the children, and teaching was also part of her duties. I can remember meeting a couple of men who signed their name with an 'X.' They couldn't read or write. I met them when they came to vote in an election, and in Australia voting is compulsory. I had to take them aside and read out the paper and mark the ballot paper as they wanted.

In some areas where there are ten or more children, a school is established by a State Government, which meets all the costs involved. Henry Lawson wrote a poem about 'The Old Bark School.'

It was built of bark and poles, and the floor was full of holes

Where each leak in rainy weather made a pool;

And the walls were mostly cracks lined with calico and sacks -

There was little need for windows in the school.

In such a school most children rode their horses and left them in the school paddock during the day, ready to ride in the afternoon. Today some might drive an old car to get to the school. They don't drive on public roads but across paddocks. I have known of some young students who drove to school in a sulky (horse-drawn vehicle), but these all came from the homestead area and were the children of the families employed on the sheep run or cattle station.

Now the Government is responsible for the education of all youngsters, so Correspondence Schools were established. Children received their lessons by post and returned their work to be marked by the teachers of the Correspondence Schools. However, the outback children missed out on a lot that city children had.

In 1944 Miss Adelaide Miethke visited Alice Springs as part of a delegation studying the work of the Flying Doctor Service. During her time in the outback she noticed how shy many children were and wondered what could be done to help them. She knew the value of the radio to call the Flying Doctor and began to make plans to use the radio to help in the education of those youngsters living in the outback.

On 8 June, 1951 the first radio transmission took place to those in the outback. There were just three lessons, each lasting only thirty minutes, which were broadcast on Monday, Wednesday and Friday between 10:00 am and 10:30 am. The subjects were Social Studies, Word Building, English language exercises, and the reading of stories. The broadcasts were made from the staff-room in a school at Alice Springs.

At first the children listened to the teacher, but with improvements in radio communication they began to take a more active part. There was a 'Trouble Corner' time when a student could talk privately to his teacher about difficulties he or she was experiencing. The Governess or parents who taught their children, could make use of the ten minutes allocated to each child. The lessons were based upon those received from the Correspondence School. All the children of the outback could be involved if they had the radio. Aboriginal children living near the homestead were also able to take part in the lessons. One problem faced by many Kooris was that English was their second language after their native tongue. In the year 2000 there were 36 aboriginal children receiving lessons through the Correspondence School and the School of the Air.

From the very start there was still the problem of loneliness, and it was decided to have a 'Get Together' at Alice Springs during one of the school holidays. The first one was held in 1955. The young people who attended, met their teacher and the other children they had spoken to over the radio. Gradually the shy youngsters became more involved in the activities, and everyone had a great time!

In 1957 the first excursion was held and eighteen children accompanied by the teacher and four adults made their way to Adelaide. Three years later one teacher set out on a 'Patrol' to visit as many families as he could. He used his own car and spent a week in the outback. Of course in a week he couldn't visit every child, but what was started, grew. Now the 'Patrol' uses Government supplied cars, and teachers who set out four times each year for a two weeks' visit to the children in the School of the Air. In 1974 the School of the Air became independent and school numbers began to grow. In 1975 there were 123 students and all were in Primary School.

In 1993 with satellites overhead it became possible for students in senior classes to use laptop computers to download lessons. All students used the Toshiba machines.

Lessons were also sent by e-mail and fax. The new inventions in communication are being widely used, but satellite communications are limited due to the cost. Today most children are involved in half hour lessons each day, plus a ten minute 'personal' time with the class teacher in Alice Springs. The lessons follow up the work set in the correspondence lessons that are done by the children.

In the year 2000, while Queen Elizabeth II was visiting Australia with Prince Phillip, they travelled to Alice Springs where they spoke to many young people using the radio.

Many times the teacher in Alice Springs introduces the children to someone with great skills, such as Midge Coleman who is an excellent potter, living in Alice Springs. He decided to have a wall at the School of the Air Centre covered with tiles made by the Primary Class people. This was to be ready by the year 2001 which marked the fiftieth year of the radio

School. The youngest kiddies were to mould hands and feet upon their tile, while Upper Primary were to produce tiles dealing with transport, the environment or technology. When they were finished the tiles were carefully packed and posted to the class teachers at Alice.

At the beginning of the 21st century the School of the Air served more than one thousand students in twelve schools. There are lessons even for pre-schoolers! Every effort is made to get the youngsters together for some activity. Each year there is an athletics carnival, held at Broken Hill, and currently about one hundred and forty children attend, many travelling long distances to take part in the events. Some travel over four hundred kilometres to be present and enjoy the day. Those present do everything town children do at their annual Athletics Carnival. Of more importance than the carnival is the opportunity for the isolated children to mix with others. The School serves an area of almost one and a half million square kilometres; one child being just over one thousand kilometres from Alice Springs. A school magazine is published for all the students enrolled in the school.

We must study hard and learn if we are to progress in the modern world. Wth the Correspondence Schools, the Radio School of the Air plays a big part. Most parents who supervise their children's lessons, listen to the broadcasts in order to reinforce what is taught.

All parents should teach their children about God. We read in Deuteronomy 6:4-9 'Hear, O Israel: The LORD our God, the LORD *is* one! You shall love the LORD your God with all your heart, with all your soul, and with all your strength. And these words which I command you today shall be in your heart. You shall teach them diligently to your children, and shall talk of them when you sit in your house, when you walk by the way, when you lie down, and when you rise up. You shall bind them as a sign on your hand, and they shall be as frontlets between your eyes. You shall write them on the doorposts of your house and on your gates.'

The prophet Ezra devoted himself to the study of God's Word and he obeyed it. In the book of James we are told that we should not just listen to God's Word but do what it says. But in order to be able to obey God's Word we must know what God is saying so do not forget to give time to the study of God's Word.

The Swagman

Some years ago Australia adopted a new national anthem in place of 'God save the Queen.' The song chosen was *Advance Australia Fair*. However, many people wanted to have a song using Banjo Paterson's poem *Waltzing Matilda*, which was a song about a Swagman:

'Once a jolly swagman camped by a billabong;

Under the shade of a coolabah tree;

And he sang as he tucked that jumbuck in his tucker bag,

Who'll come a waltzing Matilda with me.'

The song went on to tell of the swagman stealing the sheep that had come down to the billabong for a drink. He put the sheep in his tucker bag, saying: 'You'll come a-waltzing Matilda with me.'

In this poem you have already met strange words that are well-known to most Australians. You might try to work out what they all mean.

I want to tell you about men who roam about in the

outback regions of Australia - the Swagmen. There are not so many swagmen about today as was the case when I was a child. The 'swaggie' was a man who for some reason decided that the city life was not the place for him; maybe he couldn't get work or simply didn't want a job that required him at the office every day. There were a lot more swagmen in the days before the Government made Social Security payments to unemployed people. When a swaggie called at our home I always wondered where he'd been and where he was going. To my brother and me it seemed that they must have had an interesting life, doing as they pleased and going wherever they wanted to.

The swagman carried everything he owned with him in his 'swag.' He would have his possessions wrapped up in his blanket - this was his *Matilda*. In order to keep it dry on rainy days he had a tarpaulin sheet wrapped around it.

He carried some flour and salt with which to make some damper - bread without yeast. Usually he had no butter, but always carried Golden Syrup.

Somewhere safely tucked away in his swag he carried some tea and sugar. In his hand or tied to his swag was a good sized billycan in which he boiled water for his 'cuppa.' Tucked away somewhere he carried a battered frying pan or saucepan.

All of this was the swaggies' *Matilda,* which he carried as he wandered (waltzed) about. And in those days, before scientists proved that smoking was bad for our health, he usually had a cigarette between his lips. I can remember one swagman who could blow rings of smoke from his mouth; my brother and

I just watched in amazement.

Another item of clothing that marked out the men from the outback and especially the swaggies was their hat. We have plenty of flies in Australia and most homes have fly screen doors and windows to stop the pests getting inside the house. The swaggie invented a hat to keep the flies away from his face.- a hole was punched every 4 or 5 cm around the brim, through which a piece of string was fastened. Attached to each string was a cork hanging about 10 cm below the brim. As he walked along the corks bobbed about, keeping the flies from his face. Corks were ideal as they didn't hurt when they hit his skin.

The swaggie usually wore Blucher boots with good nails in the leather sole to make them last a long time. Do you know why they have this name? Of course he had his trousers, socks, shirt and a cardigan, all given to him by kind people he met on his travels.

He slept under bridges, beside rivers or billabongs (small lagoons) - anywhere he felt safe to cook a meal, find drinking water and have a wash and shave. Many years ago when rabbits were to be found in their millions, the swaggie usually carried several rabbit traps with him so he could catch bunnies for a meal. Rabbits are good eating and even today they can be purchased from some butchers.

Most swaggies had 'a man's best friend' trotting along beside him - usually a blue cattle dog. These dogs are bred in Australia to work on cattle and sheep stations. They have a set of very sharp teeth and are loyal to their owner.

The swaggie was always on the lookout for a home where he could call and ask for a meal and some flour, salt, tea and tobacco. Usually he met the lady of the house and when he had finished asking for the supplies he needed, he would offer to do some work: 'If you like Missus, I'll cut the firewood or clean up the garden. I'll do whatever jobs I can for you.'

It was often a mystery that the swagman always seemed to know which house was the best for a free meal and handout; but it wasn't long before the people of the outback discovered a white stone on the top of a fence post along the road and near the home of the generous family. It was his way of telling his mates to call and ask for supplies.

This was the Australian swagman who was part of our outback life. He had no home to call his own and he usually passed by never to return. This was like Abraham, a nomad who lived in the land of Canaan which God had given him, but at that time he could not call it his own. Abraham looked for a better home than his earthly one, a home built by God for the saints (Hebrews 11:8-16).

Christians are pilgrims on this earth. It is not our eternal home. We are just passing through, on our way to heaven, to live forever with our Saviour. Jesus walked the roads of Israel, but had nothing to call his own. On one occasion he said, 'Foxes have holes and birds of the air have nests, but the Son of Man has nowhere to lay his head' (Matthew 8:20).

However, there are great differences between Christians and the swaggie - he wears his old, worn-out clothing which can be seen, while Christians are dressed in the perfect

righteousness of the Lord Jesus which is seen by God. We should always remember that the Lord looks upon the heart!

The swagman has a dog as his friend, but our great Friend is Christ, the Son of God. The Scriptures speak of this Friend: 'But there is a friend who sticks closer than a brother' (Proverbs 18:24). We don't have to beg for spiritual food as a swaggie begs for food for his body - we have the Bible and our spiritual food is found there. We should read our Bibles and meditate upon the truth we find in it. We should attend worship where we are fed spiritual food.

When the swagman dies there is usually no one to weep his passing. However, the death of God's people is special to their Saviour. The Psalmist writes: 'Precious in the sight of the LORD is the death of His saints' (Psalm 116:15).

The saints are pilgrims, but unlike the swagmen they can always say: 'The best is yet to be!'

The Postman

The small country town where I live has mail delivered five days a week. The 'postie' rides his motor scooter and is dressed in a special uniform. When he has delivered all the mail to people on his run, he goes home as his work is complete. Only mail is delivered and rarely does he collect mail to be taken to the Post Office to be posted.

My wife, Valerie, and I can remember mail being delivered three times a week only to the farms by someone who also delivered fresh bread. He used his car to get around as his run was over many miles. He made sure that the farmers received the bread orders that they placed in the local town.

The outback mailman delivered the mail, which was only a small portion of what he delivered. Before aeroplanes were used, mail was delivered by the postman who drove a truck. He needed a truck to carry everything that the families needed to survive. Because of the size of his run he probably called in two or three times a week.

Somehow you must try to imagine the great expanse of the Australian outback. I recently read of the wife of a cattle station owner who needed urgent dental treatment. She backed out the car and drove for four and a half hours to reach the small town where the dentist had his surgery. I can drive to the local dentist in about 5 minutes.

Before aeroplanes were used the mailman took the goods that were needed by people on his run - spare parts, fresh vegetables, fruit, bread, medicines, lessons for those doing correspondence school work, petrol for machines and anything else that was needed. The mailman had a timetable to follow, but punctures, getting bogged in the sand and breakdown problems meant that he might never arrive on time. Letter boxes were often found many miles from where the people lived, and his delivery was only twice a week. Having something special to deliver he would sometimes drive right up to the homestead where he would be welcomed and invited in for a drink and a meal. There were times when the precious cargo was ruined on the way to the delivery point. One writer commented on the time when the mailman's dog made a bed out of the bread and on another occasion a hole in the drum of petrol ruined a lot of cargo.

Today people still live in the outback and the mailman makes his regular deliveries of mail and all the other goods that are asked for by those living inland. The difference now is that aeroplanes are used to cover the distance quickly. So you can see, the postman delivers more than just the mail. Anything that is needed outback will be delivered if it can fit on a Cessna 210, a Piper Cherokee, or some other small plane. Of course there is a fee charged for the delivery.

The aerial postman does not usually make deliveries every day, but I read of one mailman making deliveries during the Easter holiday. He flew over one thousand kilometres to make sure that those on his run received their mail and supplies when they were needed.

The mailman sets out collecting all the supplies needed by those living in the outback - even the school lessons from the Correspondence School! The aerial postie is centred in a large town or city; a place where he can better service these people of the outback. Soon his truck is full and he drives out to the aerodrome to load his plane. He has flown this route many times but knows his plane must be in tip-top order as he cannot risk crashing.

I have just read of one aerial mailman who sets out from Broken Hill to deliver mail and goods at thirty-two different places. His route is about one thousand kilometres and he leaves Broken Hill before sun-up in order to escape some of the heat. Most places where he is to set down are home-made aerodromes. Most are not fenced and have holes where the rabbits live and breed. The station owner does all he can to keep the landing area flat, so that there is no danger to the mailman and his plane. Sometimes landing is made more dangerous because cattle, sheep or kangaroos are grazing where they should not be. No doubt a low swoop over the offending animals would provide an animal-free landing strip.

Some of these landing places have a lot of mail-boxes. These are not the type that are found in townships but are made out of old refrigerators, washing machines, tanks or even a dishwasher. They have to be big enough for the mail and the goods being delivered. The first person to drive past the letter boxes would collect and deliver all he could to the people he would pass while returning home. This was another example of outback 'mateship.'

Nearly all aerial mailmen carried tourists on their plane. This gave them an opportunity to see the vast Australian interior from the air. As well, the lonely outback life of the cattle and sheep men and women was made more bearable by meeting and talking to the tourists. They were also made welcome by the people living near to each landing strip. Tourists, paying for the trip, meant that goods could be carried at a smaller fee.

Some mail and goods were for small country towns. Mail delivered to these places was then delivered by the local mailman using his car or truck. Of course these deliveries were over much shorter distances than that requiring a plane.

Some years ago a fun motorbike ride was started. Riding the normal postie scooter which has the maximum speed of about seventy kilometres an hour, the ride was to be from Brisbane to Adelaide. The trip through the outback would be an opportunity for all riders to see what the inland areas of Australia were really like. The next such ride is to be in 2004. The trips in 2002 and 2003 consisted of eighty people riding their Honda mailman scooters.

After the four thousand kilometre trip to Adelaide, the riders sold their motorbikes and the money was donated to a worthwhile charity. Fifty riders handed their bikes in to be sold, while the others gave what the bike was worth to the Rotary Clubs for use in their projects.

There can be no doubt that the outback postman is an important man because first of all he makes sure that the mail - letters and bills - gets through.

In the Bible we find many 'letters.' Can you name some of them and work out how many there are in the New Testament?

In the Bible they are called 'Epistles.' They are letters written by Paul, John, Jude, Peter and James to groups of Christian people. They are not set out like our correspondence. First the writer gives us his name, whereas we sign off at the end of our letter. God speaks to us through all the Scriptures.

If you received a letter from someone you loved I'm sure you would quickly open it and read the contents. I trust that every person who reads these words is reading the Scriptures which are God's messages to us.

John 3:16 is a precious text which you should know: 'For God so loved the world that He gave His only begotten Son, that whoever believes in Him should not perish but have everlasting life.' Another passage that should bring peace to your heart is found in Romans 5:8,9 'But God demonstrates His own love toward us, in that while we were still sinners, Christ died for us. Much more then, having now been justified by His blood, we shall be saved from wrath through Him.'

Don't forget to read your Bibles and pray that God gives you understanding of all that you read.

Droughts and Famine

Australia is a huge country of 7,686,848 square kilometres. The climate around the coastline attracts the larger proportion of the population of just over twenty million people who live on the fertile coast.

The people who live in outback Australia - beyond the 'back of Bourke' - as the outback is sometimes called - are the cattle kings and owners of huge sheep stations. It is a difficult and lonely life for most people who live in those sparsely settled areas.

You probably live in a place where you can walk to the corner shop or can be driven there in a short time. Your postie probably delivers mail five times a week and you just walk to the letter box attached to your front fence to get the letters. Your doctor lives nearby and if you are sick it is easy to see him. The hospital, chemist, school and paper shop are usually just down the street, you probably have friends nearby with whom you can play and your mum and dad can chat over the fence with your neighbours.

But this is not so in the outback of Australia. Out there, beyond the 'black stump' families live many kilometres apart from one another. Can you imagine that? You already have read of some difficulties faced by people living in Central Australia, but as you read on you will find more.

Cattle, sheep and crops need water and in much of inland Australia, rain is very scarce. Recently in New South Wales, almost the whole of the state has been declared to be a drought region. Some small, outback towns are so short of water that trains are being used to bring water for humans and animals to drink. In most outback places there are no gardens and the town swimming pool has been empty for several years. Crops for cattle are not to be found and many owners of the sheep and cattle stations have sent drovers with big herds to search for food for their animals in the 'long paddock.' The long paddock is the ground on each side of the road, and it just goes on and on for hundreds of kilometres. Even on the 'long paddock' there is little food for starving cattle.

Droughts, famine and floods go in cycles. There are years of drought and famine followed by years of good rain and an abundance of crops. Then come floods!

Dorothea MacKellar, one of Australia's great poets has written a poem titled 'My Country' which most Australian children learn while attending school:

'I love a sunburnt country,

A land of sweeping plains,

Of rugged mountain ranges,

Of droughts and flooding rains;

I love her far horizons,
I love her jewel-sea,
Her beauty and her terror -
The wide brown land for me!'

In some families living beyond the 'black stump' there are children three or four years of age who have never experienced rain; they've seen reports of rain falling on the TV news, but around their homes rain is something very strange to them.

Water in dams and billabongs dry up and become little more than boggy soil around a little pool of muddy water. As the weak cattle make their way to the water's edge many become bogged and die. The dingoes (the wild dogs of the outback) who are also looking for food, attack and kill the animals stuck in the mud. Then the eagles and crows also come along to feast on the dead and dying animals. Great cracks open up in the parched soil, creeks and rivers dry up, and frequently the strong, hot winds begin to blow the good topsoil from the outback regions towards the coast.

Occasionally in the coastal areas the sky turns red during the hot, dusty days, and everyone does all they can to prevent the dust getting into houses. It is impossible to fill every crack and soon the very fine dust begins to settle on the furniture and floor.

In the meantime food becomes scarce as families have little money to spend. During those times the children go without new clothes or toys. In some areas families have survived by eating rabbits. As the drought continues and it is impossible to find or buy feed for the animals, the cattle owners are forced to shoot some of their herds, although they do all they can to keep their prize breeding stock alive.

Drought is a tragedy in the outback!

When the rain begins to fall and the pastures turn green again it takes time and a great deal of money to restock the land. Usually after good rain the land becomes a carpet of brilliantly coloured wildflowers. That is the time when many tourists visit the inland.

Those years of drought, followed by times of plenty, remind me of the seven years that Egypt produced great quantities of grain, followed by seven years of drought. Zaphnath-Paaneah was placed in charge of the nation, being second in authority to Pharaoh. Do you remember Zaphnath-Paaneah? I'm sure you will when I tell you the name he was given by his parents, Jacob and Rachel. Zaphnath-Paaneah was the name given to Joseph by Pharaoh (Genesis 41:45).Under Joseph's rule the nation stored food during the seven years of plenty in order to have food in the days of famine.

Men in outback Australia do the same, but when the droughts last for four or five years, food for stock and humans come to an end. The Government then steps in and gives a helping hand to families, making sure that there is food on the table.

Recently on TV we saw a cattle man who had made sensible preparations for the drought he knew would come one day. He had dug a huge trench in the ground which was so long and wide that he could drive his trucks into the hole and unload feed that one day he would use for his cattle. Truck load after truck load went into the long trench and after covering the feed with plastic sheeting he graded the soil back over the top to make it airtight. The drought came and he had plenty of feed for his stock; he had made his preparations for that needy time. When other farmers saw his method of storing feed they said they were going to do the same during seasons of plenty.

In some areas drinking water for the animals is still pumped into troughs by windmills or engines from the deep, water reservoirs.

When restocking commences, governments usually lend money to cattle and sheep owners at reduced rates of interest. Sadly, many farmers are forced to go to the bank and borrow money at high rates of interest.

During severe periods of drought in the outback, farmers along the coast where crops suitable for cattle and sheep can be grown in abundance, give help to their mates inland.

In many places this is done without cost to anyone in the drought declared areas. Lucerne, and other crops are baled ready for transportation inland. Often people living in the cities and towns donate money so the crops can be transported without cost to feed the dying animals. Many times people owning semi-trailers have worked together to load the trucks and set off together for the outback. These efforts have never provided enough food for the animals, but it has been a great help. Christians and charities often make up food parcels for families who are in desperate need.

Droughts and famines are the cause of great heartache in Australia, but there is a drought and famine much worse than what I have described and that is a famine of the Word of God. In Amos 8:11 we read: " 'Behold the days are coming,' says the Lord GOD, 'that I will send a famine on the land, not a famine of bread, nor a thirst for water, but of hearing the words of the LORD.'"

Today there are many people who want nothing to do with God. They think they can live a happy, contented life, enjoying the things of the world, until the time comes when they want the Lord Jesus Christ, but many will find it to be too late. Nations decide they will have laws opposing God's law, and as the country sinks into wickedness, citizens begin to cry to God for help, only to find that He will not listen.

Our God has said very plainly: 'Because I have called and you refused, I have stretched out my hand and no one regarded, because you disdained all my counsel, and would have none of my rebuke, I will also laugh at your calamity; ... they will call on me, but I will not answer; they will seek me diligently , but they will not find me' (Proverbs 1:24-28).

Dorothea MacKellar's poem concludes with the words:

Though Earth holds many splendours,

Wherever I may die,

I know to what brown country

My homing thoughts will fly.

Australians who have travelled overseas - and my wife and I have done so - come back saying, 'It's good to be home! There's no place like Australia!'

This earth is not our home; even Australian Christians who love their country, know that the best is yet to be - our home is where Christ is!

Like the station owners who prepare for drought, you and I must prepare for that day when we die, or when Christians become the outcasts of the world. How can we prepare? We should read our Bibles, have fellowship with Christians, attend worship services and the other activities the church has for you; pray that God will give you a new heart that truly loves Him, and walk along that narrow way that leads to Paradise - heaven!

Lake Eyre

Australia is the second driest continent in the world, the driest being Antarctica where it never rains - moisture in the form of snow falls from the heavens. The average, annual rainfall for Lake Eyre is 125 mm. It is estimated that the annual evaporation rate is approximately 2.5 metres.

The Australian outback has been given several names. As I have already told you, to be in the outback is to be out beyond 'the black stump.' There is little green to be seen anywhere most of the time. The outback is where 'the crows fly backwards.' This is a strange expression, but it shows the wisdom of the crows who fly backwards to keep the dust out of their eyes! Many Australians speak of the 'red centre.' This name came into existence because of the colour of the sand and rocks in central Australia. 'Out the back of Bourke' is also a name given to the Australian outback.

When the early explorers set out to cross the nation, they came upon land they believed to be of no use to anyone. In 1840 Edward John Eyre said the central region was 'one vast, low and dreary waste.' Today [A.D. 2004], most of the region is used by cattle and sheep stations, oil and gas mining, and the Aboriginals who live there. There are four language groups in the region - the Arabana, the Kuyani, the Diyari and the Wangkangurra people. They lived off the local bird and animal life- the dingoes, snakes, emus and other birds. They knew where they could obtain fresh drinking water, having lived in the area for many centuries.

The Kooris had their own stories about how Lake Eyre was made. These talk about a young boy who chases a giant kangaroo and kills it. He then makes a lake out of the kanagroo skin. The poeple who made up these stories made them up to try and explain how things began. Though the stories are inventions the people who invented them cared about taking care of the land and the special places of interest such as mountains, rocks, animals, anything that the eye can see. Christians know that it was the power of our Creator God who made the whole world just by speaking the word. And everything he made was good, very good.

In the outback there is much to be seen and now I'd like to tell you about Lake Eyre which is 9,690 square kilometres in size. This lake is twice the size of Texas in the USA. The Lake Eyre region is now a National Park 1,349,251 hectares in size. The Branded Stilty was saved from extinction by baiting the Silver Gulls that attacked the eggs of the Stilts. The Ranger makes sure tourists treat the lake with care. Most of the time the lake is just an area of hard, dry salt which proved an ideal place for the late Donald Campbell to set a land speed record. In July, 1964 he broke the old record by driving his jet powered

'Bluebird II' at 648.6 kilometres/hour across the measured mile on the lake. Two very big sheep stations border the lake, 'Muloorina' which means 'Plenty of Tucker' and is 4,400 sq. kilometres in size; and 'Anna Creek Station' which is 30,114 sq. kilometres.

In both wet and dry times the temperature is between 40° and 60° Centigrade. Looking towards the horizon the heat shimmers across the landscape. Lake Eyre has been filled to capacity only three times since the British settlement in 1788. The flood of 1974 was the largest and scientists have estimated that the volume of water in the lake was 34 cubic kilometres; that is a huge amount of water to fall from the skies and wend its way down the many rivers that flow into the dry lake. Then it took just two years for the water to disappear. This was by evaporation and soaking through the soil and into the artesian basin which is the largest in the world. There have been smaller floods which occur about every 8 years. The lake is really two lakes - Lake Eyre North and Lake Eyre South, which are connected by a channel.

The artesian basin is estimated to hold 8,700 million megalitres - a megalitre is one million litres. It takes about 2 megalitres to fill an Olympic swimming pool. Landholders who drill for the artesian water have to bore down, on the average, about 500 metres. The catchment area of the rivers and creeks serving the lake covers an area of 1.2 million square kilometres. Lake Eyre is the 5th largest internal draining lake in the world, and some of the water from the northern catchment region takes nine or ten months to finally reach the lake, which in parts is the lowest spot in Australia - approximately 17 metres below sea level. The lake is covered with a salt crust about 46 cm thick which scientists have estimated to weigh about four hundred million tonnes.

In flood time the area bursts into colour and life. Flowers bloom and trees are given new life. The same happens in the many water holes in the rivers that feed into the lake. Fish are washed down the rivers and before long the water teems with the Bony Bream, the Hardy Head, the Finke Goby (found only in the Finke River), and the Yellow Belly. Fishermen come to the lake to catch the Yellow Belly which is a good fighting fish. Some imported fish, the Mosquito, Goldfish and carp are causing great harm to the native fish, of which there are about 33 species, two thirds of which are not found anywhere else in the world. The shrimp that are found in the water are most unusual. They hatch from hard shells and then immediately begin laying thin shelled eggs. The shrimp does not have to mate to lay fertile eggs.

A time of plenty after a time of drought is a wonderful experience. Water is used to describe many things in the Bible one of which is God himself. Jesus is described as the 'living water'. Someone who believes in God is described as being like a tree that is planted by streams of water. Water is essential for health for animals, plants and humans. Jesus, our 'living water' is essential for our spiritual lives. We must trust in him.

Many people have pet budgerigars which they keep in a small cage, but when Lake Eyre is in flood the golden coloured budgerigars are to be seen their hundreds. Many travel great distances to nest, lay eggs and produce a new generation. How do these birds along the coast know when the lake is being flooded?At this point in time (AD 2004) the answer is not known.

There can be no doubting that Lake Eyre is an unusual lake, but the Bible describes an even more unusual lake - 'the lake of fire' (Revelation 19:20; 20:10,14,15). In these passages we read a description of hell. Those people who have not repented of their sins will on the day of judgement be thrown into that lake, where they will be punished for ever. We have a loving, caring Saviour who came into this world to pay the price of sin for his people. His people are those who love him and are obedient to his commands. It was Jesus who said: 'If you love me, keep my commandments' (John 14:15). The most important commandment is to love God and people. This means to trust your eternal life to the Lord Jesus Christ.

Uluru and Bald Rock

In the story of David and Goliath we are told that David picked up five smooth stones and used just one to kill the giant. Have you ever wondered why he picked up *five* stones when only *one* was needed to kill Goliath? I believe that there was a good reason for what he did. We'll find out about that later on.

Of course none of his stones were anywhere as big as Australia's Ayers Rock or Bald Rock. Ayers Rock, is now known by its Aboriginal name, Uluru, and is found in the Uluru-Kata Tjuta National Park, in Northern Territory. It was the homeland of the Pitjantjatjara and Yankunytjatjara people. The park is now World Heritage listed. When you are looking at Uluru you know that you are really in Outback Australia!

Ayer's Rock was seen by the explorer, William Gosse in July, 1873 and named after the then Premier of South Australia, Sir Henry Ayers. In 1995 the area was returned to its original Aboriginal owners.

Uluru or as it was then named, Ayers Rock, became well

known throughout the world some years ago, because of a tragedy that happened nearby. A young couple was camping near the rock, when a dingo entered their tent and dragged off and killed their baby. By the time a search was organised it was too late. Some aboriginal trackers were called in, in an effort to discover where the dingo had taken the infant. The baby's body was never found, although many years later some of the child's torn clothing was discovered. The police believed that the mother had killed her daughter and the unfortunate mother spent several years in jail before she was pardoned and declared to be innocent. A movie film was eventually made of the story.

Uluru is a popular place for overseas visitors for several reasons.

First is its size! To tramp around Uluru you will walk 9.4 kilometres. The huge rock is 3.6 kilometres long and 2 kilometres wide. This huge stone is made of arkosic sandstone - look this word up in your encyclopaedia - and some people believe it to be the tip of a huge underground mountain. Many holiday makers set out on the long climb to the top which is 345 metres high. Steps have been cut into stone and in some places there is a chain fence to assist the person attempting the climb. The strain of climbing is so taxing that some people who have made their way up the mountain have suffered a heart attack. My daughter, her husband and one of their children visited Uluru some time ago. They found the climb to be very frightening and all did not make their way to the top.

Secondly Uluru appears to change colours during the daylight hours. At sun-up and sunset its colours are usually a golden orange colour. At other times it appears to be purple. Tourists come in their thousands each year to look at the amazing scene.

A *third* unusual aspect of Uluru is that it is a huge rock that has been thrown onto its side. Just a glance shows that the strata are vertical and not horizontal as should be the case if it was formed by layers of mud settling down over the years. Uluru was formed, hardened and then tossed onto its side by some great force. No human could have done this! The only way this could possibly happen was during the flood of Noah's day when great forces of rain and raging floodwaters encircled the earth. Because of the vertical strata formation of Uluru it is hard to believe that it is the top of a huge underground mountain.

In the Bald Rock National Park, situated on the New South Wales, Queensland border there is Australia's largest granite monolith - also the world's largest monolith. Bald Rock rises 200 metres out of the surrounding bush and land, and is 750 metres long and 500 metres wide.

Like Uluru, Bald Rock is also a popular tourist attraction.

Rocks and stones are mentioned in the Bible. I have already mentioned that David used a stone in his sling to kill the giant, Goliath. Have you worked out why David took five smooth stones and not just one? Maybe he was like the boy scouts and girl guides whose motto was: 'Be prepared.'

He was prepared if anyone else came to assist Goliath; or maybe he knew that Goliath had four brothers who might have joined in the fight.

Do you remember Peter's great confession to Christ who asked, "Who do men say that I, the Son of Man, am?" So they replied, "Some say John the Baptist, some Elijah, and others Jeremiah or one of the prophets." Jesus said to them, "But who do you say that I am?"

Simon Peter answered on behalf of the other disciples and said, "You are the Christ, the Son of the living God."

Jesus answered and said to him, "Blessed are you, Simon Bar-Jonah, for flesh and blood has not revealed this to you, but my Father who is in heaven. And I also say to you that you are Peter, and on this

rock I will build my church, and the gates of Hades shall not prevail against it" (Matthew 16:13-18).

The Church is built upon Christ whom Peter confessed to be the Son of God. Any church that is built upon this confession of faith will stand the attacks of Satan and the world.

Jesus is called a stone. In Mark 12:10 we read: 'Have you not even read this Scripture: "The stone which the builders rejected has become the chief cornerstone."' The Jews anxiously waited for their Messiah, but when he came, they put him to death. That was a terrible sin - the murder of God's one and only Son! Yet through his death he saved his people. Now every time you see a big rock you can think of Uluru in Central Australia. But always remember that Christ is the One on whom the church is built; he is the rock of our salvation!

Outback Quiz

1. What two oceans is Australia found between?

2. Who led the Israelites on their long journey?

3. How do cattle owners mark their cattle?

4. Who did God make an agreement with in Genesis 17?

5. What sheep breed did John MacArthur bring to Australia?

6. Who is the 'good shepherd'?

7. What name is given to the fence over 3,000 miles long?

8. What name is given to the city in Revelation 21?

9. Who claimed to be the first in Sydney to grow wheat?

10. What work has Jesus given Christians?

11. What is a Joey?

12. Who should we ask for help against sin?

13. Name an Australian bird who can't walk backwards.

14. In Deuteronomy who are told to teach God's Word to their children?

15. Name an aboriginal weapon.

16. Who should Christians tell about Jesus?

17. What three things help keep outback people safe?

18. Who made it possible for us to go to heaven and how?

19. How do outback children learn school lessons?

20. What prophet devoted himself to studying God's word?

21. What is the name of Banjo Patterons's poem about a swagman?

22. What two animals are mentioned in Matthew 8:20 when Jesus talks about the son of man having nowhere to lay his head?

23. Name one of the ways outback postmen deliver the mail?

24. Where can we read God's message to us?

25. 'Beyond the black stump' is another name for what in Australia?

26. How should Christians prepare for going to heaven?

27. Lake Eyre is twice the size of what American state?

28. What did Jesus say we must do if we love him?

29. Ayres Rock has two other names. What are they?

30. Who is the 'stone that the builders rejected'?

31. Have you accepted Jesus as your own Saviour?

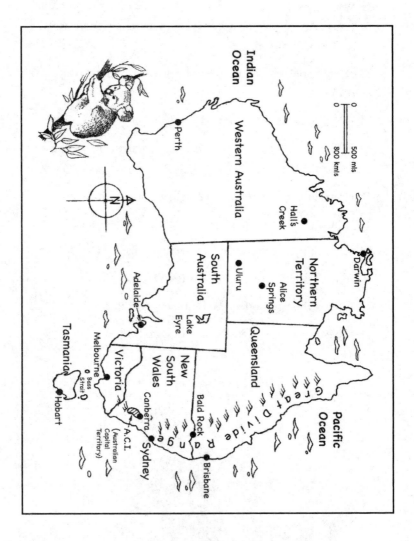

Outback Quiz Answers

1. Pacific and Indian
2. Moses
3. Branding them.
4. Abraham
5. Merino
6. Jesus Christ
7. The Rabbit Proof Fence
8. The Holy Jerusalem
9. James Ruse
10. Telling others about him
11. A baby kangaroo
12. God
13. Emu
14. Parents
15. Boomerang; spear
16. Sinners from all nations
17. Radio, aeroplanes, medicines
18. Jesus by his death on the cross
19. By radio
20. Ezra
21. Waltzing Matilda
22. Foxes and birds
23. Truck; motorcycle or motorscooter, aeroplane
24. In the Bible, God's word.
25. The Outback
26. Read the Bible, meet other christians, worship God, pray and obey God's Word
27. Texas
28. Obey his commands
29. Uluru and Bald Rock
30. Jesus Christ
31. You must answer this question for yourself.

The Adventures Series
An ideal series to collect.

Have you ever wanted to visit the rainforest? Have you ever longed to sail down the Amazon river? Would you just love to go on Safari in Africa? Well, these books can help you imagine that you are actually there.

Pioneer missionaries retell their amazing adventures and encounters with animals and nature. In the Amazon you will discover tree frogs, piranha fish and electric eels. In the Rainforest you will be amazed at the armadillo and the toucan. In the blistering heat of the African Savannah you will come across lions and elephants and hyenas. And you will discover how God is at work in these amazing environments.

Rainforest Adventures by Horace Banner
ISBN 978-1-85792-627-9
Amazon Adventures by Horace Banner
ISBN 978-1-85792-440-4
African Adventures by Dick Anderson
ISBN 978-1-85792-807-5
Rocky Mountain Adventures by Betty Swinford
ISBN 978-1-85792-962-1
Himalayan Adventures by Penny Reeve
ISBN 978-1-84550-080-1

Torchbearers
People who had courage and faith

Margaret, Agnes and Thomas have to run from the King's soldiers to live a life of danger on the hills. All Margaret wants is to make Jesus Christ the most important person in the church and in her life ... but will this conviction cost Margaret her life?

William Tyndale has enemies at every turn - even the King of England. Will he manage to get the Bible translated into the English language or will the priests and the royal household put a stop to him?

Both Margaret and William had to suffer for their faith and both paid the ultimate price with their lives - but they and others like them tell us that the truth is worth living for and dying for.

Special features:
Discussion starters, Bible Studies and 1600's timeline.

Danger on the Hill
The true story of Margaret Wilson by Catherine Mackenzie
ISBN: 978-1-85792-784-9
The Smuggler's Flame
The true story of William Tyndale by Lori Rich
ISBN: 978-1-85792-972-0

CHRISTIAN FOCUS PUBLICATIONS

Christian Focus | Christian Heritage | CF4K | Mentor

Christian Focus Publications publishes books for adults and children under its four main imprints: Christian Focus, CF4K, Mentor and Christian Heritage. Our books reflect that God's word is reliable and Jesus is the way to know him, and live for ever with him.

Our children's publication list includes a Sunday school curriculum that covers pre-school to early teens; puzzle and activity books. We also publish personal and family devotional titles, biographies and inspirational stories that children will love.

If you are looking for quality Bible teaching for children then we have an excellent range of Bible story and age specific theological books.

From pre-school to teenage fiction, we have it covered!

Find us at our web page:
www.christianfocus.com

CF4·K
Because you're never too young to know Jesus